To:

From:

OPTIMISM BY THE ACRE

OPTIMISM BY THE ACRE

Original Insights on Attitude from America's Heartland

PETER REESE

HOME • GROWN
WISDOM
C O L L E C T I O N

The cover features Lucy and Ethel, their work, the author, and his well-traveled laptop.

Photography by Kristen Boom

Copyright © 1997 by Peter Reese

Published by Garborg's Heart 'n Home, Inc. P.O. Box 20132, Bloomington, MN 55420

All rights reserved. No part of this book may be reproduced in any form without permission in writing from the publisher. Printed in USA.

ISBN 1-881830-48-9

OPTIMISM BY THE ACRE

HOME·GROWN
WISDOM
COLLECTION

*The author, a small-scale farmer whose priorities are faith,
family, and friends, dedicates this Collection to all readers
seeking SIMPLICITY, SIGNIFICANCE, and SECURITY.*

*The reader is encouraged to laugh, contemplate, and
compare experiences—and be ready to offer a differing
point of view somewhere along the way.*

OPTIMISM BY THE ACRE

HOME • GROWN
WISDOM ™
COLLECTION

*Doing what's right is
its own reward.*

OPTIMISM BY THE ACRE

HOME·GROWN WISDOM
COLLECTION™

*Ask anyone who has
accomplished anything:
None of us is as good
as all of us.*

OPTIMISM BY THE ACRE

Wisdom.
Knowledge well-composted
with humility.

OPTIMISM BY THE ACRE

HOME·GROWN WISDOM ™
COLLECTION

*Contentment concentrates
on what really is instead of
what might have been.*

OPTIMISM BY THE ACRE

The difference between an "okay" idea and a great one: The first is talked about, the second is acted upon.

HOME·GROWN WISDOM COLLECTION

Your time is your personal currency. Spend it wisely.

Reflect on the good.
Be challenged by the difficult.
Seek contentment at all times.

OPTIMISM BY THE ACRE

HOME·GROWN
WISDOM
COLLECTION™

*The best time to brainstorm
is when you have gutters
to catch the runoff.*

HOME·GROWN
WISDOM
COLLECTION ™

*Brilliance is the blazing afternoon sun,
kindness the precious candlelight in
the darkest of nights.*

OPTIMISM BY THE ACRE

HOME·GROWN WISDOM
COLLECTION ™

All those in favor of consensus
signify by saying "we."

OPTIMISM BY THE ACRE

HOME·GROWN
WISDOM
COLLECTION™

Worry.
Concern taken to an
unhealthy extreme.

OPTIMISM BY THE ACRE

HOME • GROWN
WISDOM
C O L L E C T I O N ™

*The gap between "need" and
"want" is filled with headaches
and heartbreaks.*

OPTIMISM BY THE ACRE

*Boredom is not a lack
of something to do but a
refusal to do anything.*

OPTIMISM BY THE ACRE

HOME·GROWN WISDOM
COLLECTION™

Character.
Courage under fire,
commitment over time.

OPTIMISM BY THE ACRE

HOME·GROWN
WISDOM ™
C O L L E C T I O N

Innovation.
Dissatisfaction made productive.

OPTIMISM BY THE ACRE

HOME·GROWN WISDOM COLLECTION™

*Appreciation acknowledges
the colossal impact of
one life on another.*

OPTIMISM BY THE ACRE

HOME·GROWN WISDOM COLLECTION™

Discernment is knowing right from wrong. Judgment is choosing the former over the latter.

Convictions guide our steps in the darkest nights, in the worst of weather, and whenever signposts are faint.

Those who appreciate, gain far more than they ever relinquish.

Success is not the destination,
but the effect of the journey
upon the traveler.

OPTIMISM BY THE ACRE

*Forbearance requires more strength
than the bearing of force.*

HOME·GROWN WISDOM™
COLLECTION

Wit is not a measure of the mind's depth but of its speed.

OPTIMISM BY THE ACRE

*Greatness is the power
to restrain strength.*

*Quiet is a challenge
to the busy to reflect and
to the lazy to repent.*

HOME·GROWN
WISDOM
COLLECTION™

Laughter.
A frequent guest in the
home of the contented.

OPTIMISM BY THE ACRE

*Compassion focuses on the inside,
comparison on the outside.*

*Heroes are average people
with exceptional commitment.*

OPTIMISM BY THE ACRE

*Worry never made a day last longer
or the hours go faster.*

OPTIMISM BY THE ACRE

*Anger is a proven shortcut
to long-term problems.*

HOME·GROWN
WISDOM
COLLECTION™

Ideas are never lacking.
It's the courage to do something
with them that's in short supply.

OPTIMISM BY THE ACRE

HOME·GROWN
WISDOM
COLLECTION ™

Integrity.
Colorless. Odorless.
Priceless.

OPTIMISM BY THE ACRE

To be average is acceptable.
To be mediocre, far less so.

OPTIMISM BY THE ACRE

HOME·GROWN WISDOM™ COLLECTION

Hope is a conscious decision rather than a lucky coincidence.

OPTIMISM BY THE ACRE

HOME·GROWN WISDOM

C O L L E C T I O N

Encouragement makes the path straighter, smoother, and shorter.

OPTIMISM BY THE ACRE

*Personal potential is like a hammer.
It doesn't build anything until
it's put to work.*

HOME•GROWN
WISDOM
COLLECTION™

*Encouragement costs a nickel
and yields five dollars.*

OPTIMISM BY THE ACRE

HOME·GROWN WISDOM COLLECTION

Seek and you will find.
Sit and you will forfeit.

OPTIMISM BY THE ACRE

*A disdain for humor would be funny
if it weren't so "demotivating."*

HOME·GROWN WISDOM ™
C O L L E C T I O N

Pride.
A dangerous condition brought
on by flying above a safe attitude.

OPTIMISM BY THE ACRE

Some see the glass half empty, others half full. Only a few dare to search for the pitcher that filled it. Fewer still seek the original source.

OPTIMISM BY THE ACRE

HOME·GROWN
WISDOM
COLLECTION™

Humor affirms our serious need
for a lack of gravity.

OPTIMISM BY THE ACRE

HOME·GROWN WISDOM
COLLECTION

Discontent finds company in the most expected of places.

OPTIMISM BY THE ACRE

HOME·GROWN WISDOM ™
C O L L E C T I O N

Putting the past behind requires placing the future ahead.

OPTIMISM BY THE ACRE

*Think of achievement as a process
rather than an event, a commitment
to continuity instead of a
moment of glory.*

OPTIMISM BY THE ACRE

HOME·GROWN
WISDOM
COLLECTION™

*The dreams to be pursued
still look good in the light of day.*

OPTIMISM BY THE ACRE

HOME·GROWN
WISDOM
COLLECTION™

*Celebration and sorrow
each make the other
more significant.*

HOME·GROWN WISDOM ™
C O L L E C T I O N

Freedom carries the responsibility to choose the best among the good.

OPTIMISM BY THE ACRE

HOME·GROWN WISDOM ™
COLLECTION

*It's impossible to put a dollar figure
on a sense of humor.*

OPTIMISM BY THE ACRE

HOME·GROWN WISDOM ™
C O L L E C T I O N

Laughter is one of the best medicines.
Get your prescription refilled
immediately.

HOME · GROWN WISDOM COLLECTION

Worry seeks to alter the unchangeable, control its consequences, or avoid the inevitable.

OPTIMISM BY THE ACRE

HOME·GROWN WISDOM ™ COLLECTION

*Expect nothing and receive little.
Anticipate something and be ready
for a tidal wave of response.*

OPTIMISM BY THE ACRE

HOME•GROWN
WISDOM
COLLECTION™

*Dreams are only foolish
to those who lack them.*

OPTIMISM BY THE ACRE

*Build wells to forget and bridges
to remember.*

Pessimists long for what was.
Optimists see what can be.

OPTIMISM BY THE ACRE

HOME·GROWN WISDOM

C O L L E C T I O N

Contentment is not just about where you are, but why you're there.

*Doubt is like walking through a
railroad tunnel without a flashlight.
You know daylight is ahead, but
you're tempted to go back through
the darkness to where you began.*

HOME·GROWN
WISDOM™
C O L L E C T I O N

*Fear motivates many to choose
mediocrity over the magnificent,
today's status quo over tomorrow's
opportunity, and apprehension
over adventure.*

OPTIMISM BY THE ACRE

HOME·GROWN WISDOM
COLLECTION™

Opportunity comes with obligations,
potential is realized at some
level of personal sacrifice.

OPTIMISM BY THE ACRE

HOME·GROWN
WISDOM
C O L L E C T I O N
™

*People of vision never hesitate
to use their 20/20 hindsight.*

OPTIMISM BY THE ACRE

HOME • GROWN
WISDOM ™
C O L L E C T I O N

*Determination is motivation
shifted into four-wheel drive.*

OPTIMISM BY THE ACRE

HOME·GROWN
WISDOM
COLLECTION™

*Heroes are naïve enough
to do what's right.*

*Measure a person's success not by
what they've built but by how long
it stands after they're gone.*

*Bravery is one part adrenaline,
one part foolishness, and
one part selflessness.*

HOME·GROWN
WISDOM™
COLLECTION

*Patience.
One thing nobody can get
fast enough to suit them.*

OPTIMISM BY THE ACRE

HOME · GROWN WISDOM ™
C O L L E C T I O N

Each day is a gift.
Amazingly, some exchange
it unopened.

OPTIMISM BY THE ACRE

HOME·GROWN WISDOM™ COLLECTION

*Many find humility
comes at too high a price
of submission.*

OPTIMISM BY THE ACRE

HOME·GROWN WISDOM™ COLLECTION

*Creativity is reorganizing
"what is" to construct
"what can be."*

HOME·GROWN WISDOM COLLECTION ™

The right attitude is a function of gratitude, not latitude.

OPTIMISM BY THE ACRE

Worries are like golf strokes:
Those with the fewest
are the winners.

HOME·GROWN
WISDOM
COLLECTION

*Commitment.
Hard to find, tough to keep,
easy to lose.*

OPTIMISM BY THE ACRE

HOME·GROWN
WISDOM ™
COLLECTION

Comparison is about ego.
Aspiration, about overcoming.

OPTIMISM BY THE ACRE

*Patience requires sitting still
long enough to learn the value
of sitting still at all.*

HOME·GROWN
WISDOM
C O L L E C T I O N

Creativity.
A process of eliminating the mediocre,
the familiar, and the complex.

OPTIMISM BY THE ACRE

HOME • GROWN WISDOM ™
C O L L E C T I O N

Given its apparent short supply, common sense is inaccurately named.

OPTIMISM BY THE ACRE

*Destinies take shape
one moment
at a time.*

OPTIMISM BY THE ACRE

Encouragement.
Keep dispensing it at home
even if you already gave
at the office.

OPTIMISM BY THE ACRE

HOME·GROWN
WISDOM
COLLECTION

*Extraordinary effort
transforms average to exemplary,
sufficient to superior.*

OPTIMISM BY THE ACRE

HOME·GROWN WISDOM
COLLECTION™

One day ends to give the next
a chance to start afresh.

OPTIMISM BY THE ACRE